The Path to
Sexual Healing

Other Bible studies by Linda Cochrane

Forgiven and Set Free: A Post-Abortion Bible Study for Women

Healing a Father's Heart: A Post-Abortion Bible Study for Men (with Kathy Jones)

The Path to Sexual Healing

A Bible Study

Linda Cochrane

Baker Books

A Division of Baker Book House Co
Grand Rapids, Michigan 49516

© 2000 by Linda Cochrane

Published by Baker Books
a division of Baker Book House Company
P.O. Box 6287, Grand Rapids, MI 49516-6287

Third printing, March 2005

Printed in the United States of America

ISBN 0-8010-6325-6

For current information about all releases from Baker Book House, visit our web site:
http://www.bakerbooks.com

I want to acknowledge our Heavenly Father for providing forgiveness through Jesus Christ, and the way for true transformation, and for giving us his Word as a light and the Holy Spirit as a guide.

This book is dedicated to all the men and women who went through the pilot study and lovingly submitted to the process of applying godly principles to their sexual lives. Without their perseverance, this study would never have made it.

Contents

Introduction

Jesus Christ is coming back for a bride, a bride that is pure, holy, and radiant. His bride will be beautifully dressed, without a spot, a stain, or a wrinkle. Her lanterns will be trimmed, filled with oil, and ready to light. Christ's bride will be ready. Are you ready?

The church is the bride of Christ and if you are a Christian, you are part of his church. This study is designed to prepare you for Christ's coming as your bridegroom.

Feeling like the bride of Christ may seem nearly impossible if you have been sexually wounded. Seeing yourself as holy, pure, and full of God's light does not easily follow sexual trauma, one of the most soul-staining experiences of life. When a person has been sexually defiled, he or she may feel ashamed to stand in the presence of a holy God. Sexual sin leaves darkened spots of guilt on an innocent soul, and the self-confidence of victims of sexual abuse often collapses under the trauma of defilement.

In a similar way, standing before a holy God after having committed sexual sin is a frightening prospect. Our failures exposed by the light of his presence make us want to run and hide, a normal response of our sin nature. And we often feel more guilty about sexual sin than any other, even fearing to confess it to God. We try to hide it from our fellow sinners and we act as if our sexual life is hidden from God. It is not. He sees everything and knows everything. We cannot hide our guilt and shame from our holy God. If we are to be the bride without a spot, without a stain, and without a wrinkle, we must respond to his call for cleansing. He tenderly calls to us, "Come away, my beloved." We must come out from hiding, get into his light, and face our uncleanness. There is nothing to fear when we long for his cleansing. In his forgiveness we can feel pure. In his presence we can feel acceptance.

Becoming the bride of Christ is a process of transformation. The holy Creator of our sexuality has a perfect plan for us and as he sanctifies us, we become more like the man or woman God created us to be. Being created in the image of God, we have his ways and his principles written in our hearts. We may choose to follow those ways or we may choose to go our own way. He does not force us to follow his sexual plans for us.

God's perfect plan for our sexuality is for us to remain sexually pure before marriage. And when married, we are to remain monogamous and faithful to our partner. If you are married, his plan is for you and your spouse to have sex only with each other. If you are single, God's plan is for you to abstain from sexual relations. Married or single, our thoughts, attitudes, and actions must be pleasing to God.

In God's perfect plan there is no sexual perversion or abuse. But we live in a fallen and imperfect world. This study is for those who have fallen and not followed God's perfect plan. It is also for those who have been victims of sexual abuse. The good news is God heals and forgives. If we know God's standards—and we do because God's ways are written on our heart—we know where we have fallen short. The negative impact of sexual sin on our soul is extensive, but there is a remedy. This study will help you find and apply that remedy.

God sees our sexual expression in marriage as a serious commitment and he wants to deepen our love and affection for our spouse as we grow older. God's plan is that our love for our spouse will grow out of our love for God. If we commit ourselves to God and follow him with devotion, we will want our sexual life in line with his plans for us, a plan that is holy and pure and follows his ways. The sexual union in marriage is an act of worship to a holy God.

Sometimes people isolate their sexual life into a compartment separated from the rest of their life. God wants the whole of our life devoted to him. He wants our sexuality to reflect his presence in our life.

There are consequences for ignoring God's perfect plan and going our own sexual way. Sexual sin is a sin against our own body and it is in our body that we bear the consequences of our sexual sin. There are also spiritual consequences to sexual sin. These consequences touch our soul. When we keep our sexual life separated from God, there are negative spiritual results that remain in our heart.

This Bible study looks at the spiritual consequences of sexual trauma and sexual sin. The goal is to allow the window of our soul, with all its pain and impurities, to be opened to God. In Scripture we find our God is one who longs to heal our wounds and purify our defilement.

This study is for the victim of another's sexual sin as well as for the one who has committed sexual sin. It is for anyone who has ever gone his or her own sexual way and is now ready to go God's way.

We are living in a time when sexual sin is ravaging the souls of our families. Incurable venereal diseases are on the increase. Date rape has violated the innocent. The wombs of women are being scarred by abortion. Uncommitted sexual relationships bear children with no roots or families, as men are losing their incentive to protect and provide for their offspring.

Dangerous abusive and stalking behaviors are on the increase. Infertility is on the rise due to undetected, untreated sexually transmitted diseases. Sexual assault has become so commonplace that we are no longer astounded by its epidemic proportions. Wounded people are turning to members of their own sex for comfort and safety only to find the emptiness of the homosexual lifestyle. Feeling hopeless about ever developing a truly loving relationship, many of us settle for something much less and miss God's best for our sexuality. God's desire for all his married children is that a tender, enduring love deepen through the years. And for his single children, God desires that they celebrate the blessings of the single life.

As the sexual revolution totters along, its crippled and maimed veterans are finding their way to our churches. We as a church must be ready to minister to those devastated by sexual sin in the world or in their own homes. Children of God are not exempt from the pain of sexual sin. They too can victimize or be victims of sexual abuse and violence. Being a Christian does not guarantee protection from being raped or abused. The church can welcome and care for the victimized. The church can help those who are guilty of sexual sin to repent and be cleansed.

It is my prayer that this study will deepen your knowledge of the perfect plan God has for your life. May you know the conviction and the comfort of the Holy Spirit, the forgiveness of our Savior Jesus Christ, and the healing offered through his Word.

How to Use This Book

This Bible study can be used in small, confidential study groups as well as in Christian counseling and ministry settings. It is recommended that the individuals or group meet weekly. Individuals should complete the lesson on their own before coming to the group session. Group leaders may want to allow some time at the beginning of each session for participants to share how the things they are learning impacted their lives during the previous week. There are also questions provided at the end of each lesson for group discussion.

There is no leader's guide needed for this study because each question and Scripture builds on the previous question and each chapter relates to the preceding one. The questions are based on the New International Version of the Bible. Participants should write insights, commitments, and prayers on the pages provided at the end of this book or in a separate journal.

Because the subject is an emotional one, it may be difficult to do this study alone without the support of a group or counselor. The questions remind us of times we would rather forget. If you attempt to do this study alone and find that strong emotions arise, consider seeking professional Christian counseling. If you are determined to plow through this study on your own, enlist the support of a prayer partner. Choose someone with whom you can be honest and who will be honest with you.

This study is a good place to start for those who desire to be free from the consequences of sexual trauma. It will minister to those who have wandered in the wilderness of sinful sexuality too long and now want to know the way home. Urging change, transformation, and repentance is the deep and often painful work of the Holy Spirit. This study is for those who want to submit to the Holy Spirit's profound work of transformation, who want to learn God's way of sexual holiness.

As Christian men and women allow God's Spirit to work in them, cleansing and transforming them, Christ's radiant bride will indeed be ready and waiting for her bridegroom. Christ's bride will be men and women standing in purity and walking in holiness.

Whom have I in heaven but you?
  And earth has nothing I desire besides you.
My flesh and my heart may fail,
  but God is the strength of my heart
  and my portion forever.

                                    Psalm 73:25–26

I pray also that the eyes of your heart may be enlightened in order that you may know the hope to which he has called you, the riches of his glorious inheritance in the saints, and his incomparably great power for us who believe.

                                    Ephesians 1:18–19

One

A Relationship with God

Do you know God? Do you really know him? Often the God of our thoughts is not the God of reality. Before we can experience God's healing of wounds caused by sexually traumatic experiences, we must know him, the one who created us. How is this possible? In the Bible we see who God is. His character is revealed in the pages of his Book, which encourages us to know him and get close to him. This means we must talk to him, ask him questions, listen to his answers, and follow his instructions.

In loving relationships, we are drawn to spending time with the person we love. Discovering new things about those we love and getting to know them on a deeper level is a joy. Developing a relationship with God is a joy also. Knowing that his heart is inclined toward us helps us to trust him. Understanding who he is helps us feel safe with him. When we stop the flurry of empty activity and sit and listen, we hear his loving call, "Come away, my beloved." Talking to him about the consequences of sexual sin is the beginning of healing as the deeply painful areas of our sexual lives are comforted in his presence. Responding to his call, we begin to get to know the one who heals.

Knowing Him

We can know about God or we can know him. Most everyone knows about God but fewer people know him. Do you want to know *about* him or do you want to *know* him? Knowing him means entering into a love relationship with the one who created you. Look into the following Scriptures to discover how you can know God.

1. Who did God tell Moses he was in Exodus 3:13–14?

2. What does this mean to you?

3. What do the following Scriptures encourage you to do to know God?

   Psalm 25:4

   Psalm 46:10

   John 14:21

4. What did the Lord tell Jeremiah he would do to help his people know him? How would knowing God change his people (Jeremiah 24:6–7)?

5. What are the benefits of knowing God?

   John 10:14–16

   John 17:3

1 John 4:7

6. What effect did knowing God have on the apostle Paul (Philippians 3:8)?

7. What are the results of *not* knowing God (2 Thessalonians 1:8)?

8. Is it possible to convince God that you know him when you really don't (Matthew 7:21–23; 2 Timothy 2:19)?

9. What is a sign of not knowing God (1 John 4:8)?

10. When you think of getting to know God or getting to know him better, what goes through your mind? What are some of your fears? What are your hopes?

11. On a scale of one to ten, how much would you like to know God?

1	2	3	4	5	6	7	8	9	10
not very much									*more than anything*

Where on this scale do you want to be?

12. What do you plan to do to reach this goal?

13. What do you think God is asking you to do so you will know him or know him better?

14. God has always known you and he knows all about you (see Psalm 139:1–4). How does the realization that God knows about your sexual sins and the sexual damage you have suffered make you feel?

15. Spend fifteen minutes sitting quietly and thinking about the verses you have read. Ask God to show you his will for your knowing him. Write out your impressions at the end of the fifteen minutes.

Knowing His Love

Everything we have ever needed in a love relationship will be met in a relationship with Jesus Christ. The love we need is fulfilled in him. The approval and the attention we long for is satisfied in his presence. The sense of belonging we crave is answered when we become his child.

When we accept God's gift of salvation, he establishes a covenant relationship with us, made possible through the death and resurrection of his Son, Jesus. This covenant will never be broken. God never breaks up with, separates from, or divorces his people. What amazing love he has for us! The following Scriptures will help you discover more about his unfailing love.

1. How is the love of God described in the following verses?

   Exodus 15:13. The love of God is _____.

   Psalm 118:1–4. The love of God _____.

   Numbers 14:18. God is _____ in love.

   1 John 4:8. God is _____.

2. Which of these characteristics would encourage you to talk with God about your sexual life? Write out your prayer below, asking God to help you now.

3. Have you ever felt that God's love failed you? Write about it briefly, stating what you felt.

4. What does 1 Corinthians 13:8 state about God's love failing you?

5. What does God promise to those who love him?

   2 Chronicles 6:14

   Nehemiah 1:5

6. According to the previous Old Testament Scriptures what are the conditions God sets for him to keep his covenant?

7. In the New Testament Jesus establishes a new covenant. What do you have to do to share in the new covenant (John 3:16)?

8. Will your covenant relationship with God ever be broken?

   2 Corinthians 1:20

   Hebrews 7:21–22

9. A covenant is "a formal, solemn, and binding agreement." What would you say is the difference between a covenant relationship and a noncovenant relationship? Give an example of each.

10. Have you ever broken your covenant relationship with anyone? What happened?

11. Has anyone broken his or her covenant relationship with you? What happened?

12. Have you ever felt separated from the love of God? What was your situation at that time?

13. What does Romans 8:38–39 state about being separated from God's love?

14. Write a prayer in the space provided below, telling God how you feel about getting to know him and getting close to him. Tell him how you would feel talking to him about your broken covenant relationships.

15. What would you like God to do for you in this study? What changes would you like to see in yourself? Write your goals below.

Group Discussion Guide

Scripture Memory Verse

Be still, and know that I am God.
Psalm 46:10

Discussion Questions

1. How does a person get to know God?
2. What stops most people from knowing God?
3. What would it take for you to believe that God loves you?
4. What do you want God to do for you in this study?

Righteousness and justice are the foundation of
    your throne;
  love and faithfulness go before you.
Blessed are those who have learned to acclaim you,
  who walk in the light of your presence, O LORD.
They rejoice in your name all day long;
  they exult in your righteousness.

Psalm 89:14–16

"For I know the plans I have for you," declares the
LORD, "plans to prosper you and not to harm you,
plans to give you hope and a future."

Jeremiah 29:11

Two

Resting in a Holy God

How do you feel about bringing your sexual experiences before a holy God? In this study you will be encouraged to take your intimate struggles to the Lord. Approaching him with experiences that bring feelings of shame and guilt will take great effort but it is important to be open and honest with God. It will take considerable courage not to hide from his holiness, which is our natural tendency when we have strong feelings of shame or guilt. We will want to keep a safe distance from God when we are tormented by thoughts of our unworthiness.

How can you get past the overwhelming feelings of condemnation? Start by getting alone and being still. Look into his Word. Call out to him in honesty. Persevere. He wants you to come to him with all of your sexual shame and guilt. Don't let your fear prevent your fellowship with him.

This study will encourage you to draw near to God. You will find that you can trust him, that you are safe and secure in the circle of his holiness. Look into the following Scriptures to discover more about God's holiness.

Holiness

1. Think back to when you were a child. What were you taught about holiness?

2. What things were considered holy?

3. Were there any people you thought were holy?

4. The word *holy* means "exalted or worthy of complete devotion as one perfect in goodness and righteousness; divine; sacred." How was your understanding as a child different from the dictionary definition of holy? How was it similar?

5. As an adult what do you consider holy?

6. If you commit yourself to God and follow him with devotion, you will want your sexual life in line with his plans for you. Sometimes people isolate their sexual life, keeping it separate from the rest of their life. God wants all of your life, including your sexual life, devoted to him. Is there anything in your life that God would consider unholy?

7. What words did the characters in the following Scriptures use to describe God?

   Mark 1:24

   John 6:69

   Revelation 4:8

8. How did Isaiah feel in the presence of a holy God (Isaiah 6:1–5)?

9. How do you obtain confidence to go before a holy God?

   Hebrews 10:19–23

   Hebrews 4:15–16

10. How do you feel when you realize that the holy God knows all about your sexual thoughts and sexual behavior? How do you think he feels about it?

11. As you think about God knowing all about your sex life, what do you want to say to him about it? Write out your thoughts in a prayer below.

12. As God's children we are to become more and more like him, participating in his holiness. How does this happen (Hebrews 12:10–11)?

13. When we put ourselves under God's control, we reap a benefit that leads to holiness. What is the result (Romans 6:19–23)?

14. Can a person be moving toward holiness and have a sex life at the same time? Explain your answer.

Wounded by Sexual Sin

When we engage in sexual sin or sexual sin is forced on us, we are left with the sad consequences—wounds to our bodies and our souls. Sexual sin damages the soul and it is a sin against our own bodies. Sexual sin that is forced on us leaves us feeling ashamed and defiled. When we initiate sexual sin, we suffer guilt. In either case, our soul is left crushed and broken.

God is able to heal this damage. The following questions are designed to help you identify where sexual sin may have wounded your soul. Pray for guidance as you answer these questions honestly. Don't spend time thinking about each question before answering. Give your first yes or no response. If you are doing this study with others, share only the answers you are comfortable sharing.

1. Do you have difficulty expressing yourself sexually?
2. Do you avoid times of intimacy?
3. Do you struggle with lust?
4. Do you sometimes feel powerless to assert or protect yourself against sexual harm?
5. Do you feel unworthy of being loved or cared for in the way you need?
6. Do you struggle with eating too much or too little?
7. Do you feel ashamed of your body?
8. Do you view your body as dirty, ugly, or bad?
9. Do you have difficulty believing your body is a home for the Holy Spirit?
10. Have you ever used drugs or alcohol as an emotional pain reliever?
11. Have you ever needed to use drugs or alcohol to be able to express yourself sexually?
12. Do you have any self-punishing behaviors?
13. Have you ever chosen sexual partners outside of God's plan? Remember, God's plan is no sexual partner until marriage and then your spouse as your only sexual partner until death.
14. Have you ever been a victim of another person's sexual sin?
15. Do you have a general mistrust of men or women?
16. Are you tempted with sexual perversions?
17. Are there any areas of your sexuality that are not in line with God's plan?

18. Has your sexuality ever gone to the extremes of promiscuity or frigidity?
19. Do you struggle with memories of past sexual sin?
20. Are you aware of suffering from any consequences of your own sexual sin?
21. Do you have habitual and progressively worsening destructive sexual habits?

Look back over your answers. For each yes response, try to determine if the behavior is a consequence of your sexual sin and list it in the space below. If it is a consequence of being a victim of another's sexual sin, list it under the second heading below.

Consequences of my sexual sin:

Consequences of being subjected to someone else's sexual sin:

Soul Repair

Regardless of how much you have been wounded by sexual sin, God can restore your soul. He specializes in repairing soul damage. Even if you answered yes to all the questions in the previous section, there is help. No matter what has been done to you or what you have done, God can bring you to a place of purity.

To find God's purity we must want to change. Healing comes to those who are desperate for change and recognize the need for deliverance. Desperation looks like surrender. Often people know they are in bondage and want to be free but they are not desperate enough to surrender. Desperate people confess their brokenness to one another. They help one another in their need to be free. Recognizing that they are in bondage, they surrender to God's will. People desperate for God want to obey him at all costs to their pride. And as they cry out to God, he delivers them.

He answers their cry and then carries them to a place of rest and trust in him. Look into the following Scriptures to discover God's plan for soul restoration.

1. As you read Psalm 42 record what the psalmist did to allow God to repair his soul.

    verses 1–2:

    verses 3–4:

    verses 5–6:

    verses 7–8:

    verses 9–11:

2. What did the psalmist do when his soul was downcast (v. 5)?

3. How and where does God restore your soul (Psalm 23:1–3)?

4. Where can your soul find rest?

    Psalm 62:1, 5

    Matthew 11:28–30

    Hebrews 4:9–11

5. To have rest you must go to God alone. You must go and place your cares at his feet. In a practical sense you need a quiet place in your life, a place where you can be alone and undisturbed with God, a private place for restoration. This is difficult if you live with others. You may have to train those you live with to allow you a place of refuge. Help them under-

stand that you need this for your spiritual health. Describe below the quiet place you have or will create for yourself.

6. Here are two examples of God's telling his people to rest. Read the Scriptures and record what they were instructed to do to find rest. Then record what the consequences of *not* resting were.

	Instructions for Rest	Outcome of Not Resting
Isaiah 28:12–13		
Jeremiah 6:16–19		

7. How did David feel after resting his soul (Psalm 131:2)?

8. What are the fruits of resting in the Lord?

   Isaiah 30:15

   Isaiah 32:17–18

   Isaiah 40:29–31

9. Check which of the following are fruits of resting in the Lord:

   ❑ renewed strength
   ❑ decreased feelings of weariness
   ❑ increased power
   ❑ finding repentance and salvation
   ❑ more peace
   ❑ more confidence

10. Describe the last time your soul felt rested. Where were you? When was the last time you experienced the fruits of restoration? What was the experience like?

11. God commands us to rest. If we don't rest in him, all our work will come to nothing. We will feel as if we are taking one step forward and two steps back. In rest, we find God and his heart of love for us. We find confidence and strength. We find peace. In our rest we find our source of power, and our weariness is removed. Why do you think rest is so important for healing your wounds caused by sexual sin?

12. What is your plan for allowing God to restore your soul? Write it out in a prayer below.

Group Discussion Guide

Scripture Memory Verses

He makes me lie down in green pastures, he leads me beside quiet waters, he restores my soul.

Psalm 23:2–3

Discussion Questions

1. How do you feel about bringing your intimate struggles to the Lord?
2. What areas of your sexuality need God's healing?
3. How does God repair our souls?
4. Can a person have a sex life while moving toward holiness? Explain.

Oh, the depth of the riches of the wisdom and
  knowledge of God!
How unsearchable his judgments,
  and his paths beyond tracing out!
Who has known the mind of the Lord?
  Or who has been his counselor?
Who has ever given to God,
  that God should repay him?
For from him and through him and to him are all
  things. To him be the glory forever! Amen.
                              Romans 11:33–36

Three

God's Perfections

God is perfect in his love toward us and when we are in his presence, we are safe. Being in his perfect presence is different from being in the presence of a perfectionist, who demands perfect behavior and is unforgiving toward those who make mistakes. Perfectionists are not safe. God encourages his perfect ways but is forgiving and merciful toward those who fall short of these ways. Look into the following Scriptures to learn how to feel safe in the presence of a perfect God.

Perfect in Character

1. Fill in the blanks to discover what aspects of God's character are perfect.

   Deuteronomy 32:4. His _____ are perfect.

   2 Samuel 22:31. His _____ and _____ are perfect.

   Romans 12:2. His _____ is perfect.

   Job 37:16. His _____ is perfect.

2. What other aspects of God's character are perfect?

   Psalm 50:2

   Isaiah 25:1

   1 John 4:18

3. Which of these aspects of God's perfections do you find easy to believe? Which do you find the hardest to believe?

4. If you believe God's character is perfect, as the Scriptures say, will your experiences in your sexual life change in any way? If so, how?

Perfect in His Work

God is perfect in his ways, his knowledge, and his will for our sexuality. If we truly believe he is perfect in faithfulness and love, we will trust his ways. We will come to him with our pain and heartache and find his will for our healing. If we trust that he is perfect in his work in us, we will come to him with our tainted sexual lives and find hope for change.

1. What does God's Word teach about perfection (2 Corinthians 13:11)? How does this affect your sexuality?

2. Does God expect us to aim for perfection and holiness?

   Matthew 5:46–48

   1 Peter 1:15

3. How are we to aim for this perfection?

   Philippians 2:5–6

   1 John 3:16–18

4. God has a perfect plan for your sexuality that is pure and holy. Whether you are married or single, your thoughts, attitudes, and behavior can be pleasing to God. How do you feel about aiming for God's perfect plan for your sexuality?

5. If you are ready to commit your sex life to God's direction, read 1 Corinthians 10:31 and use it to guide your prayer to God for his help. Write your prayer below.

Jesus Never Fails

Almost everyone has had at least one person give him or her the wrong message about sex. Rarely does anyone escape exposure to wrong sexual behavior. We are subjected to warped messages about sex everywhere we turn and the majority of us have never received any godly messages about sex. We have learned that sex is bad. We have been entrusted to the care of abusers. We have been subjected to the behavior of those who have perverted their authority and used sex to hurt us. Never having heard the truth, we continue in familiar sinful patterns. Never having had healing from damaging sexual experiences, we continue to react as if the damage were still taking place.

Victims of sexual sin sometimes blame God for the horrible things that have happened to them. They believe God has failed them and they blame him for sending the trauma their way. The truth is that the trauma they experienced was not initiated or blessed by God—allowed, yes, but not ordained by him. Because we live in a fallen world with people who behave in a fallen manner, we know people who choose to selfishly use and hurt one another. People will fail us, but God will never fail. It is impossible for his love to fail because that's his nature—God is love. He is the only one who will be faithful to us. The only one who will never fail is Jesus.

1. Read the Scriptures to discover what characteristics of God never fail.

   Isaiah 51:6. His _____ never fails.

   Lamentations 3:22. His _____ never fail.

   1 Corinthians 13:8. His _____ never fails.

   1 Kings 8:56. His _____ never fail.

2. If love never fails and God is love, you can trust his unfailing love. God's unfailing righteousness will help you in the areas where you have failed in your sexual life. You can be assured his unfailing compassion will heal your sexual wounds. What part of God's unfailing character do you need most at this time in your life?

Perfect Promises

People lie; God tells the truth. People break promises; God keeps his promises. God is faithful to keep all his promises to us. All his promises are yes in Christ (2 Corinthians 1:20). We can be strong and courageous when we know God will not fail us. We can go forward and do the work involved in our healing, trusting that he will complete the process. He will not abandon us in the middle of our pain. His mercy will not allow our sexual sins to destroy us. We can trust his promises.

1. What kind of promises does God make?

   Joshua 21:45

2 Peter 1:4

2. When God makes a promise, does he keep it? Always? Look into the following Scriptures concerning God's trustworthiness.

Numbers 23:19

Psalm 145:13

2 Corinthians 1:20

3. In the Bible God made many promises to various people who followed him. Because God is unchanging, we can claim many of those promises for ourselves. What promises does God make in the following verses?

Deuteronomy 4:31

1 Chronicles 28:20

Psalm 89:28

4. Which promises of God are the easiest for you to believe? Which promises do you find difficult to believe?

5. Record three of God's "great and precious promises" for you (you may want to refer back to the first two chapters of this study):

-

-

-

6. How do the promises of God affect the life of a believer?

   Psalm 119:148

   2 Corinthians 7:1

   Hebrews 10:23

7. When we have the promises of God in our hearts, we want to purify ourselves from everything that would contaminate our bodies and our spirits. We want to be rid of sexual impurity. We find hope in his promises and meditate on them even in the night. Even in the times we fall into the pit of despair over what we have done, we choose to hold on to hope. On a scale of one to ten how difficult is it for you to believe God's promises?

1	2	3	4	5	6	7	8	9	10
very difficult									*very easy*

8. Are you where you would like to be in trusting God's promises? If not, where would you like to be and what is your plan for getting there?

Our Attitudes about Sex

We learn our sexual behavior from birth. Every sexual experience shapes our thoughts and actions. Every positive or negative message we receive forms our view of our sexuality. We receive most of our training about sex from our parents, even if sex was never spoken about in our homes. Attitudes, behaviors, and the purposes of sex are all expressed explicitly or tacitly in the home.

The next section will help you look at what you learned about sex growing up. Answer the questions honestly. It is more important to answer them honestly than to not answer them for fear of exposure. They are between you and the Lord. If you are doing this study with others, share only those answers you feel comfortable sharing.

1. What did you learn from your mother about being a woman?

2. What did you learn from your father about being a man?

3. What did you learn from your mother about sex?

4. What did you learn from your father about sex?

5. What did you learn from your brothers about sex?

6. What did you learn from your sisters about sex?

7. What did you learn from your uncles about sex?

8. What did you learn from your aunts about sex?

9. What did you learn from your cousins or any other relatives about sex?

10. What did you learn from childhood friends about sex?

11. In what areas of your sexual life have you experienced failure?

12. Do you think the messages you received from others contributed to your failure? Explain.

13. What did you learn from your religion about sex? Did your religion fail you in this area? Explain.

14. What did you learn from your church about sex? Did your church fail you in this area? Explain.

15. What did you learn from your culture about sex? Did your culture fail you in this area?

16. What did you learn from your race about sex? Did your race fail you in this area?

17. What did you learn from your school about sex? Did your school fail you in this area?

18. What do you think was the most powerful message you ever received about sex?

19. It's often difficult to rid our minds of wrong attitudes we have held for years. Think about what would happen if you got rid of all the wrong messages you've received about sex. How would your sexual life change if you believed God would never fail you? How would your sexual life change if you believed God would keep his promise to be with you always? How would your sexual life change if you really believed God loves you and made you a sexual being?

Scripture Memory Verse

> Since we have these promises, dear friends, let us purify ourselves from everything that contaminates body and spirit, perfecting holiness out of reverence for God.
>
> 2 Corinthians 7:1

Discussion Questions

1. How can you feel safe in the presence of a perfect God?
2. What were you taught as a child about being perfect?
3. How do you feel about aiming for God's perfect plan for your sexuality?
4. Will Jesus ever fail you?
5. What does God promise you?

God is our refuge and strength,
  an ever-present help in trouble.
Therefore we will not fear, though the earth give way,
  and the mountains fall into the heart of the sea.
Psalm 46:1–2

Blessed is the man who trusts in the LORD,
  whose confidence is in him.
Jeremiah 17:7

Four

God Is Faithful and True

Knowing God and knowing his unfailing love is the start of the healing process. Trusting God with our damaged sexuality is the key to transformation. As we entrust to him our sexuality, he will show us how to grow in purity. His Holy Spirit will convict us of sexual sin and grieve with us over it. He will cry with us over the wrongs we have done.

God also comforts us in the pain of past abuse, when we were sexually used. His heart breaks over the things that were done to us.

Trusting God does not mean that horrible things will never happen again or that we will never sin again. But when we entrust ourselves to his care, we never again have to go through anything alone. He is with us, showing us the way out of abuse and out of temptation.

God brings his children to a place where they learn to trust him alone. When we put our trust in people, we set ourselves up for failure. When we place our confidence in anything other than the Lord Jesus Christ, we will often experience heartache. But in God we experience blessings as we learn obedience and find that he keeps his promises. In him we have freedom from self-centeredness and fear and so we are able to build loving relationships.

When major relationships break down, people tend to withdraw and not trust anyone. But when we have a stable, loving relationship with God, we are able to build stable, trusting relationships with our fellow human beings.

We can't trust God, however, until we know him. Look into the following Scriptures to discover more about the loving, trustworthy, unfailing character of God.

Where Is Your Trust?

1. Read Revelation 19:11–16. Jesus is the rider on the white horse.

   What is he called in verse 11?

   What name is written on his thigh?

   What do these names tell you about the trustworthiness of Jesus?

2. Look at the following verses to see where God encourages you to put your trust. Then note the results of trusting in these areas.

	Area of Trust	Result of Trusting
Psalm 13:5		
Psalm 20:7–8		
Proverbs 3:5–6		

3. The name of Jesus is Faithful and True. His character is unfailing love. When we put our trust in the Lord, we will rise up and stand firm, rejoicing in our salvation. When we acknowledge his ways, he will guide and direct our path. Using the following Scriptures, discover the benefits of putting your trust in the Lord.

Nahum 1:7. He _____ those who trust in him.

Romans 10:11. Those who trust in the Lord will _____ _____.

Romans 15:13. To those who trust him, he gives _____ _____.

4. Trusting in the Lord means we are in his care. The following Scriptures warn against putting our trust in the world. Read the Scriptures and record what is not to be trusted and the result of trusting the things of the world.

	What We Trust	The Result
Psalm 20:7–8		
Psalm 146:3–4		
Proverbs 11:28		
Isaiah 47:10		

5. The only one we can put our total trust in is God. Choosing to trust someone who is not trustworthy can bring heartache. Who was betrayed in the following Scriptures?

Psalm 41:9

Luke 22:21–22

6. People will betray our trust. God will never deceive us or betray our trust in him. When we trust in people, God cannot save us. All our plans will come to nothing. Trusting in the things of the world will lead to our own destruction. Where have you put your trust—in power, money, other people? What have

you experienced when you trusted in the things of the world? How did this type of trust affect your sexual life?

7. How did you feel when you found your trust in someone was unwarranted? Are you still trusting someone who is not trustworthy with your sexual life? What do you need to do about it?

The Years the Locusts Have Eaten

Anyone who suffers trauma will experience its long-term effects. Those who have been injured in a car accident respond with fear in near-accident experiences. Survivors of a fire often overreact when they sense a fire hazard. It is the same with sexual trauma. The effects of abuse and sin will remain long after the experience. Negative emotions will be triggered by subsequent sexual encounters. We carry the weight of each sexual experience in our memory. We react to godly sexual experiences as if they were unsafe. We respond to impure sexual situations as if they were familiar. Have you been living with the consequences of sexual trauma?

It will take acknowledgment of the trauma to bring about remedy. Understanding the trauma helps us recognize and understand our later responses. Facing the consequences will allow God to heal the wounds. The questions that follow will help you think about the past. Record your first response to each question. Be honest. Do not minimize the effect of sexual trauma. Let God show you what he wants to heal.

Trauma is defined as a disordered psychic or behavioral state resulting from mental or emotional stress or physical injury. Considering this definition, answer the following questions.

1. What sexual trauma did you experience as a child?

2. What sexual trauma did you experience as a teen?

3. What sexual trauma did you experience as a young adult?

4. What sexual trauma did you experience as an adult?

5. Which of these experiences caused you the most trauma?

6. In which of these experiences were you the victim?

7. Which of these experiences were caused by your own sin?

8. What trauma from these experiences would you like God to heal?

9. Read Joel 2:18–27 about God's promise to restore Israel and write out what you would like God to restore for you.

10. Do you trust God to restore the "years the locusts have eaten" (v. 25)?

Trusting God with the Past

Do you want God's healing and deliverance? You must trust God with the truth of your personal history, believing that he won't reject you because of it. Choosing to trust God is a step of faith, a step of obedience. Even if every relationship in your life has failed you, you must push past the doubt that God will be unfaithful to you. He is worthy of your trust. Until you trust God with your past, you cannot trust him for your future. But when you begin to trust him, he will guide you in growing to trust him more.

Look into the following Scriptures to discover more about God's trustworthiness.

1. What is worth trusting?

   2 Samuel 7:28. God's _____ are trustworthy.

   Psalm 19:7. God's _____ are trustworthy.

   Psalm 119:86. God's _____ are trustworthy.

2. Describe a time when you found God trustworthy in your personal life.

3. In what areas does God promise faithfulness? What is the condition for experiencing his faithfulness?

	Promise of Faithfulness	Action on Your Part
2 Samuel 22:25–26		
Psalm 25:10		
1 John 1:9		

4. Summarize the previous Scriptures by completing the following statement.

   When I _____, God will _____.

5. Because God is faithful, what can we trust him to do for us?

   1 Corinthians 1:8–9

2 Thessalonians 3:3

6. What kind of character does a faithful God have (Deuteronomy 32:4)?

7. When we trust God as our Savior, we receive many benefits. God forgives our sins and protects us from the harm of the evil one. What can those (the unfaithful) who don't trust God expect?

   Proverbs 11:6

   Proverbs 13:2

   Proverbs 13:15

8. People who don't know God are trapped by evil desires and they crave violence. Their way is hard. Was this what your life was like before you became a child of God?

9. What can we expect as Christians when we don't trust God?

   Jeremiah 3:19–21

   Matthew 6:30–32

   1 John 2:15–17

10. What are the benefits of being faithful to God?

    Psalm 31:23

    Proverbs 2:8

    Proverbs 28:20

11. When we are faithful, we come into God's protection and blessing. What does it mean to be faithful to God in your sexual life?

Trusting God for Healing

1. Will you choose to trust God to heal you of the trauma of your sexual experiences?

2. Write out three reasons you are able to trust him.

    I am able to trust God and be honest about my sexual experiences because . . .

    I am able to trust God to forgive my sexual sin because . . .

    I am able to trust God to heal my past because . . .

3. Write out three ways you plan to be faithful to God this week.

    I will be faithful to God by . . .

    I will be faithful to God by . . .

    I will be faithful to God by . . .

Group Discussion Guide

Scripture Memory Verse

In repentance and rest is your salvation, in quietness
and trust is your strength.

Isaiah 30:15

Discussion Questions

1. What is worth trusting?
2. When we put our trust in some things, it leads only to heartache. What are some of those things?
3. How have traumatic experiences affected your sexuality?
4. What does it mean to be faithful to God in your sexuality?

In the same way, count yourselves dead to sin but alive to God in Christ Jesus. Therefore do not let sin reign in your mortal body so that you obey its evil desires. Do not offer the parts of your body to sin, as instruments of wickedness, but rather offer yourselves to God, as those who have been brought from death to life; and offer the parts of your body to him as instruments of righteousness. For sin shall not be your master, because you are not under law, but under grace.

Romans 6:11–14

But grow in the grace and knowledge of our Lord and Savior Jesus Christ.

2 Peter 3:18

Five

Changing Your Mind

Daily we are bombarded with lies about healthy sexuality. To focus on what God says about sex is a struggle. But we must decide whether to believe the world's message about sex or to believe God's message. His plans, his ways, his principles for our sexuality are struggling to have their way in our life. How we think about sex greatly influences how we behave sexually. To have godly behavior, we must have godly thoughts. Do you want the mind of Christ for your sexuality? The next section will guide you. Change will occur when the way you think about sex becomes the way God thinks about sex.

What I Think about Sex

Let's begin by looking at what thoughts about sex are in your mind right now.

1. Complete the following statements with the first thought that comes to your mind.

   Sex is . . .

   Sex is . . .

   Sex is . . .

   Sex is . . .

   Sex is . . .

   Sex is . . .

   Sex is . . .

2. Female sexuality is . . .

3. Male sexuality is . . .

4. I want my sexual thoughts and actions to be . . .

5. The one thing I want to learn is . . .

6. The one thing I need to change is . . .

Changing My Mind about Sex

As we have said, the way to change your mind about sex is to have new thoughts. Our thoughts must line up with God's thoughts. We cannot have true sexual healing apart from having the mind of Christ. God wants to transform us into something new. He wants to change our sexuality into something beautiful for him, a sweet fragrance of his glory. Look into the following Scriptures to learn the difference between a mind controlled by the Spirit and a mind controlled by the world.

1. Where does sin start (James 1:13–15)?

2. According to verse 15 what is the final outcome of thinking about sin?

3. On what is the spiritual mind set (Romans 8:5–6)?

4. On what is the natural mind set (Romans 8:5–6)?

5. What are some of the characteristics of the mind of a sinful person (Romans 8:6–8)?

6. According to Ephesians 4:17–19, what happens to the thoughts of an unbelieving heart?

7. The desire for sin starts in our minds. Evil thoughts and wrong desires lead to wrong actions. Wrong actions lead to tainted character. Tainted character leads to the death of our spirit. God wants to change our minds to save our souls. Personalize the following Scriptures by filling in the blanks.

Romans 12:2. God wants to transform me by _____ so I will be able to _____.

2 Corinthians 3:18. God wants to transform me into _____ so I will reflect _____.

Philippians 3:21. God wants to transform my _____ into his _____.

8. Summarize the previous Scriptures by completing the following statements.

God wants to transform me by . . .

When I am transformed I will . . .

9. To be transformed into God's likeness, we must have our minds renewed so that we no longer conform to the world's pattern of thinking. This is God's way of holiness and purity. What is the first step for gaining control over your thoughts (2 Corinthians 10:5)?

10. What kind of thoughts would you consider obedient to Christ?

What kind of thoughts would you consider disobedient?

11. To be obedient to Christ's teaching, what specific thoughts of yours would you like to take captive?

12. What is God's plan for your making your thoughts new?

Ephesians 4:22–23

Philippians 4:8

Hebrews 4:12–13

A New Mind-Set

God wants his children to have control of their thoughts. He doesn't want us to let our thoughts wander aimlessly, ending up in vain imaginings and evil desires. The Bible says that when we get to heaven, we will give an account to God of our thoughts.

What kinds of thoughts does God want us to have? Philippians 4:8 says that we should think about things that are pure, lovely, and praiseworthy. How do we know that our thoughts are not pleasing to God? If our conscience doesn't tell us, then the Word of God will. God's Word is able to penetrate our thoughts. When we read it, our thoughts are judged.

When we desire to change our thoughts, God will help us. He can lead us in having a new mind-set or attitude. He can give us a desire to have pure thoughts, if that is what we want. When we start changing our thoughts, we will see changes in our behavior. When our changed behavior becomes a habit, we see our character transformed and set free of the bondage of evil thoughts. In this way we become more like Christ.

It is important to focus on your sexual thoughts in light of what God desires for you. Are they impure? If so, they need to be changed.

1. Name three things you want to change your mind about regarding your sexuality.

    •

    •

    •

2. Write a prayer asking God to renew your mind and change your thoughts about sex.

Group Discussion Guide

Scripture Memory Verse

Do not conform any longer to the pattern of this world, but be transformed by the renewing of your mind. Then you will be able to test and approve what God's will is—his good, pleasing and perfect will.

Romans 12:2

Discussion Questions

1. What does it mean to change your mind about sex?
2. What is God's plan for changing your mind?
3. What are the benefits of having a restored mind?
4. What will happen if your mind is uncontrolled?

I will give you a new heart and put a new spirit in you; I will remove from you your heart of stone and give you a heart of flesh. And I will put my Spirit in you and move you to follow my decrees and be careful to keep my laws.
Ezekiel 36:26–27

Blessed are the pure in heart, for they will see God.
Matthew 5:8

Six

A New Love Song

The Song of Solomon is a love song. Often called the Song of Songs, it is the book of the Bible that God filled with his word on romantic relationships. It is the story of a love relationship ordained by God and celebrated by friends. There are three voices in this book: the groom or lover, the beloved or the bride, and the friends who celebrate their love. The book describes the courting relationship of two people in love, Solomon and the Shulamite woman.

The Song of Solomon has been interpreted in various ways. There are many questions about who this love story is really about. Does it simply describe the relationship between two lovers? Or is it the story of the relationship between Christ and the church? In this study we will think of it in both contexts. Christ loved the church, so he compares his relationship with the church to a relationship between husband and wife. As we have seen, the church is his bride, and he has a covenant relationship with her, like the marriage covenant that binds a husband and wife. It is an agreement to be one, to be united in mind, body, and spirit.

If we are united with Christ in a covenant agreement, then we must be pure. That includes our relationships and our sex life. There is no allowance for perversion in our relationship with Christ. If we indulge in perversions, our intimacy with God is inhibited and our relationships with family and the church are imperiled. Perversions also defile our nation.

Song of Songs reveals truths about ourselves and our relationships to one another, truths that will aid in restoring our hearts to purity in the realm of sex. These Scriptures will replace old thoughts with God's new thoughts.

If your sex life has been impacted by the world's way of thinking, Song of Songs will be difficult reading. Your heart may absorb only a little bit of truth at a time. It may take many readings before you are able to receive even one verse of truth. But keep at it, praying for the Holy Spirit's enlightening.

Reading Song of Songs

1. Read 2 Timothy 3:16. What is Scripture used for?

2. Is Song of Songs included in this list? Explain.

3. Read Song of Songs every day and when God says something to you about loving, intimate relationships, record it. It may be difficult at first to understand what God is saying, but continue to read until God speaks to your heart. Meditate on these Scriptures until you can apply them to your life in a practical way. When reading Song of Songs, ask yourself these three questions:

   • Is there any area of my thinking in the area of sex that needs correcting?
   • Is there anything in the area of sex that I need training in?
   • Is there anything in the area of sex that I need rebuking in?

Day 1
   What I read:

What God said:

Day 2
What I read:

What God said:

Day 3
What I read:

What God said:

Day 4
What I read:

What God said:

Day 5
What I read:

What God said:

A Hardened Heart

Hearts damaged by sexual trauma are like beautiful flowers crushed under the heel of Satan. Only God can restore the broken petals, making us beautiful again with a fragrance he treasures. Since God created sex, he knows how to heal us when we suffer the wounds of sexual trauma. As he heals us and changes us, we will learn to take great delight in him and his gift of sexuality. Whereas formerly we may have viewed our sexuality as a curse, we will begin to see it as a blessing.

The healing process is important because we tend to harden our hearts when we are hurt, and hardened hearts turn away from God. Hardened hearts that have not learned to forgive develop bitter roots that damage the whole body. As we envelop ourselves in bitterness, our relationships suffer, our bodies suffer, and our deep needs go unmet.

The good news is that God wants to heal us, and, if we want to be freed, he can free us from bitterness As God purifies and softens our hearts, we develop a strong desire to follow in his ways. As he forgives us and teaches us to forgive the ones who hurt us, we find that forgiveness is a balm for our hardened hearts.

Look into the following Scriptures to learn about hardened hearts.

1. Read the Scriptures and record whose heart became hard and for what reason. What effect on their lives did their hardened hearts have?

	Who	Reason for Hardened Heart	Aftereffects
1 Kings 11:4–11			
2 Chronicles 36:11–13			
Hebrews 3:15–19			

2. How do hearts become hard?

Isaiah 6:8–10

Ephesians 4:18

Hebrews 3:15

3. How are hearts softened?

   Ezekiel 11:17–19

   Ezekiel 18:31

   Ezekiel 36:26

4. How would you assess the condition of your heart? Is it soft toward God and his ways? Are there any areas, particularly in your sexual life, where your heart is hard toward God?

Remember to read Song of Songs each day and record your thoughts in the space provided at the beginning of this chapter.

A Broken Heart

1. In Psalm 109:21–24 what is the condition of David's heart?

   Where does he go for help (v. 26)?

2. Where is God when his children are feeling brokenhearted (Psalm 34:18)?

3. What is God's desire for the brokenhearted?

   Psalm 147:3

Isaiah 61:1–3

4. What do you think is the difference between being hard-hearted and brokenhearted?

5. How does God respond to the brokenhearted?

Psalm 51:17

Isaiah 57:15

Matthew 11:28–30

6. How does God respond to the hard-hearted (Zechariah 7:8–14)?

7. When we are brokenhearted about our sin, what does God do?

Psalm 51:12

Psalm 145:18–19

8. When we remain hard-hearted, what happens?

Psalm 95:8–11

Proverbs 28:14

9. What sexual experiences in your life broke your heart and drew you closer to God?

10. What sexual experiences in your life hardened your heart and drew you away from God?

Remember to read Song of Songs each day and record your thoughts in the space provided at the beginning of this chapter.

A Pure Heart

1. In Psalm 51:10–12 David describes the kind of heart that God desires for us. What kind of a heart is that?

2. How does God respond to the pure in heart?

   Psalm 73:1

   Jeremiah 24:7

   James 4:8

3. What does a pure heart produce (1 Timothy 1:5)?

4. What does God promise to the pure in heart (Matthew 5:8)?

Remember to read Song of Songs each day and record your thoughts in the space provided at the beginning of this chapter.

A Changed Heart

1. What has led you into sexual sin in the past?

2. Have any of these sins left your heart wounded? What areas of your heart need healing?

3. What benefits did God's people experience when they turned to the Lord? Finish the following statements.

   Deuteronomy 4:29–31. If they _____ with all their heart, God would _____.

   Deuteronomy 11:13–14. If they _____ the Lord with all their heart, God would _____.

   Deuteronomy 30:2–3. If they would _____ to the Lord with all their heart, God would _____.

4. What can we expect when we trust in the Lord (Proverbs 3:5–6)?

5. What do you believe is God's desire for your sexuality?

6. What steps do you need to take to follow God's plan for your sex life?

Group Discussion Guide

Scripture Memory Verse

> Create in me a pure heart, O God, and renew a
> steadfast spirit within me.
>
> Psalm 51:10

Discussion Questions

1. What do you think of the relationship between the bride and groom in Song of Songs?
2. What is the difference between being brokenhearted and being hard-hearted?
3. How does God purify hearts?
4. How does God bless us when we turn to him with our whole heart?

Do you not know that your body is a temple of the Holy Spirit, who is in you, whom you have received from God? You are not your own; you were bought at a price. Therefore honor God with your body.

1 Corinthians 6:19–20

You are all sons of God through faith in Christ Jesus, for all of you who were baptized into Christ have clothed yourselves with Christ.

Galatians 3:26–27

Seven

Changing Your Clothes

Our clothes reflect who we are; they tell our story. Clothes can mirror our nationality, race, occupation, religion, and even our sexual identity. One of the first things parents notice when their children start to develop sexually is a change in their clothes. Their clothes reflect their sexual culture.

God wants our exterior to reflect who we are in him. We are to clothe ourselves with compassion, kindness, humilty, gentleness, and patience (Colossians 3:12–13). In this chapter we will not only look at changing our spiritual clothing but consider changing our physical clothing if it is not pleasing to God. When we come to Christ, we take off the world and wrap ourselves in God's style. We take off the old clothes with their old ways and step into his garments and his new ways. Everything about us, including our sex life, should reflect who we are in him.

God has guidelines for our garments. Wearing what is pleasing to God is more than the length of our skirt or the fit of our pants. When we are in love with Jesus Christ, we dress as his bride. Our image must be holy, pure, radiant, and full of his glory.

We become aware of every spot, stain, or wrinkle and are convinced of the need to change. As the inner self changes to mirror God in us, we shed what is not becoming and are attracted to garments that say we are his child.

Physical and Spiritual Nakedness

1. In the beginning, in the Garden of Eden, Adam and Eve were naked. What were their feelings about being naked (Genesis 2:25)?

2. What happened when they sinned and how did their feelings change (Genesis 3:7–10)?

3. What was their first reaction to their nakedness (v. 7)?

4. Imagine yourself standing naked before God. How would you feel? What would you want to cover?

5. God is more concerned with our inner self than with our physical body. When the Old Testament speaks of God uncovering the nakedness of people, it means that he is exposing their sin. What reasons are given for people being uncovered in the following Scriptures?

   Isaiah 47:1–6

   Ezekiel 16:35–38

   Nahum 3:5

6. In the Old Testament when God was angry with his people, he exposed their sins. People try to cover their sins and hide from God and from each other. What does Hebrews 4:13 say about hiding our sin from God?

7. If we do not turn from our sexual sins, God may choose to expose them. We have a choice: Take off our old self with its sinful ways or be uncovered and exposed; humble ourselves before God or be humiliated before people. God will uncover areas of rebellion in our life. What things in your life would you like to keep covered?

8. When we commit sexual sin, God doesn't always uncover it and expose it immediately. If we are not instantly struck by lightning, we may think we got away with our sin and we test God and do it again. He sometimes lets us go a long way before we feel the consequences of sexual sin.

It is to our advantage not to wait until the lightning strikes. God's desire is for us to choose to uncover our sins and confess them to God. Look into the following Scriptures to see what God wants us to do.

Ephesians 4:22–25

Take off:

Put on:

Colossians 3:5–9

Put to death or get rid of:

Put on:

James 1:21

Get rid of:

Accept:

9. By committing ourselves to Christ, we take off the old self
   and put on the new self. This new self represents Christ and
   his holiness and his righteousness. We put to death the
   things that are sexually immoral. We get rid of all evil and
   accept God's Word as the truth. What are some things from
   your old self and sexual life you are still wearing? What things
   would you like to take off? Write out your prayer below.

Under God's Fountain

God created sex. It was his idea. Sex is not evil or bad or wrong
or dirty. Sex is a gift from God that he created for marriage. Unfor-
tunately the world has perverted God's beautiful gift of sex, using
it with impure motives for selfish and evil intentions. Sex has
become a commodity, used to gratify self, exercise power, and
manipulate others. Because the world's view is so prevalent, it's
difficult to feel good about sex, to remember that it is a beautiful gift from God. Even Christians may feel that their sex life in
marriage is somehow tainted and impure.

God's Word can help us feel clean again. By understanding
God's purpose for sex, we can feel like his radiant bride, standing in purity and walking in holiness. God will bless our sex life
when it is what he intended it to be—used exclusively to give
pleasure to our partner in marriage. God will help us keep our
sex life pure; he will help us with self-control.

The Bible teaches that God blesses the sexual act, the intimacy
it creates, and the children it produces (Genesis 1:28; 2:24; Song

of Songs 1:12–16; 1 Corinthians 7:3–5; Psalm 127:3–5). If there is doubt in your mind about sex and its goodness, his Word will help you see the truth. Coming to understand that God intended sex for pleasure in marriage may take time but it will come as you grow in faith. If your sexuality is out of control or you have shut down your sexual needs, read God's Word and believe the truth.

1. In Leviticus 16:29–30 the Israelites cleansed themselves on the Day of Atonement. From what were they cleansed?

2. How do we receive cleansing for our sins today?

   Titus 3:3–6

   1 Corinthians 6:11

3. The death of Christ has atoned for our sins once for all. Now we go to him for cleansing from all our impurities. Read Hebrews 9:13–14. How are we cleansed?

4. Something impure is lewd, unchaste, or containing something unclean or foul. Whatever is impure needs to be made pure. From what do you need to be purified?

   Jeremiah 4:14

   2 Corinthians 7:1

   1 John 1:9

5. Through the blood of Jesus, we are purified from anything that contaminates our bodies and our spirits. Imagine your-

self under a fountain of God's cleansing water. What impurities would you want him to cleanse?

6. When we confess our sexual sin, we accept God's cleansing. What areas of your sexuality do you feel are contaminated? What areas would you like to have God purify?

7. You must confess to God any sexual sin, so that you may feel sexually pure. Write out your prayer of confession below.

Putting On New Clothes

When we confess, we are cleansed. When we repent, we accept Jesus' payment on the cross for our sin. When we receive Christ as our Savior, his death and resurrection bring us into God's kingdom and we submit to the cost of discipleship. Discipleship teaches us new ways to live. The old ways don't fit. The old clothes don't feel right anymore. Therefore we change our soiled clothes for immaculate attire. Then, standing in purity and walking in his holy ways, we represent our King. We are his ambassadors. We are precious daughters and noble sons of the King.

1. As a child of the King, what "clothes" are you to put on?

   Isaiah 52:1

   Isaiah 61:3, 10

Romans 13:14

Colossians 3:12–13

1 Peter 5:5

2. We clothe ourselves with our Lord Jesus Christ. We put on his character of love, kindness, humility, and compassion. We put on his garments of praise and array ourselves in his robes of righteousness. Are there any garments you are still wearing that represent your old sexually sinful ways or the negative ways you thought about your sexuality? What clothes (attitudes and behaviors) do you think God might want you to change? What do you plan to do with this clothing?

3. To be sexually pure takes commitment. It takes great strength to resist old familiar patterns that are prevalent in the world. It is essential that we protect our purity from the enemy. What type of protective clothing will you put on?

Romans 13:12–14

Ephesians 6:11–18

1 Thessalonians 5:8

4. We put on the whole armor of God. We protect our sexuality with his armor of light and love. If we remember we are wearing the helmet of salvation, it is harder to fall into sin. When we wear a breastplate of faith, we will not fear the enemy's fiery darts.

Sometimes those who have been sexually traumatized try to hide their sexuality. They fear falling into sexual sin so they make themselves asexual. They may choose to wear unflattering clothes that hide their masculinity or their femininity. Pray and ask God to show you where you may be hiding in fear. Write your prayer below.

5. Is there anything you wear now that makes you feel more like a woman of God or a man of God? Consider the clothes in your closet. What do you wear that increases your sense of being a precious child of the King? Is there a possibility you need some new clothing to reflect your new and purer attitudes toward your sexuality?

6. Draw a picture of you wearing your new clothes.

Group Discussion Guide

Scripture Memory Verses

You were taught, with regard to your former way of life, to put off your old self, which is being corrupted by its deceitful desires; to be made new in the attitude of your minds; and to put on the new self, created to be like God in true righteousness and holiness.

Ephesians 4:22–25

Discussion Questions

1. When Scripture says that we are uncovered and naked before God, what is meant?
2. What is the reaction most people have when they fall into sexual sin?
3. How are people cleansed from sexual sins?
4. What type of "new clothes" does God want us to wear once we have been cleansed?

Do not love the world or anything in the world. If anyone loves the world, the love of the Father is not in him. For everything in the world—the cravings of sinful man, the lust of his eyes and the boasting of what he has and does—comes not from the Father but from the world. The world and its desires pass away, but the man who does the will of God lives forever.

1 John 2:15–17

Humble yourselves before the Lord, and he will lift you up.

James 4:10

Eight

Turning Around

If we change our mind about sex and begin to believe what God says about sex, we will not continue in our old sinful patterns. After we begin to think pure and holy thoughts about sex, the old thought patterns don't fit. We turn around and go another way. When we change our mind, our actions want to follow, but that is when the struggle begins. Our flesh wants to stay trapped, continuing in old destructive patterns. Change is painful, fearful, and fills our hearts with anxiety. The old ways are familiar; sinful ways are easy. The new way of repentance is unfamiliar but it is necessary if permanent change is to take place. Repentance is the way God transforms lives. Look into the following Scriptures to discover why repentance is necessary for healing you of sexual sin.

The Meaning of Repentance

1. The dictionary gives three definitions of *repent*:

    —to turn from sin and dedicate oneself to the amendment of one's life

—to feel regret or contrition
—to change one's mind

With which of the dictionary definitions do the following Scriptures agree?

Acts 3:19

Acts 26:20

2 Corinthians 7:10–11

2. In repentance we turn to God. Our sins are wiped out and our behavior reflects our turning. We then feel refreshed knowing we are cleansed and free. What feelings accompany repentance (2 Corinthians 7:10–11)?

3. What is the difference between "worldly sorrow" and "godly sorrow"?

4. Many of the prophets were told to warn God's people of the need to repent. As the prophets identified with the people in their need for repentance, what feelings were expressed?

Ezra 9:5–6

Jeremiah 14:20–22

Jeremiah 31:19

5. In repentance there is a sense of shame for the acts committed against God. There is a fear of the sexual sin bringing dishonor to the name of Christ. Repentant people have a sense of humiliation and disgrace. They fear God's disapproval and beg for his forgiveness. Read the following verses to discover the process involved in repentance.

Acts 11:21–23

Acts 20:21

2 Corinthians 7:8–11

True Repentance

In turning to God in repentance, there is a type of sorrow. This sorrow may be caused by our confronting our sexual sin. If it is godly sorrow—a sorrow that produces an earnestness and an eagerness to do the right thing—the sorrow will bear the fruit of righteousness. Godly sorrow leads to life.

1. How does God respond to a repentant heart?

   Isaiah 19:22

   Isaiah 30:15

2. When we need God, we turn to him. Sometimes this need is the consequence of our sexual sin. When we turn to God, he promises to hear our cries and to heal us. God responds to a repentant heart by providing rest and quietness. What did Jesus say about repentance?

   Mark 1:15

Luke 15:10

3. Have you responded to Jesus' call for repentance? If so, explain how.

4. What do the following verses encourage someone who has repented to do?

Acts 2:38

Acts 26:20

5. What do you need to repent of in your sexual life?

6. Of what sexual sins would you like to see your family repent?

7. Of what sexual sins would you like to see your church repent?

8. Of what sexual sins would you like to see your nation repent?

Godly Sorrow

When we hear that prominent Christian men and women have been involved in sexual sin, we are crushed. The public exposure harms the name of Christ and brings discouragement to those who believe in the power of repentance.

Long before public exposure, however, a loving God has encouraged the sinner to stop his wrong behavior. Bringing conviction and warning, he uses many avenues to bring his people to private repentance before there is public humiliation. Humility before God is a much better choice than humiliation in public. When the sinner is in need of forgiveness, God, unlike most people, is always ready to supply it. The public has a low tolerance for sexual sin among people who call themselves Christians. And even brothers and sisters in Christ are often hesitant to forgive.

Christians, however, must be ready to minister to those who have been ensnared in the devil's trap. We need to help bring reconciliation to those who have been damaged by the abuse of sex in our culture today. We must be available with consistent Christian accountability. Repentant people need others to counsel them and ask them the hard questions. They need true Christian fellowship that will encourage their hearts daily. They need people to pray and intercede for them. Those who have escaped the snare of sexual sin should look around them in their own churches and be sensitive to others who are hurt and searching for the way. Christians who have struggled with sexual sin and found victory will be able to comfort others with the comfort they have received from God.

There is hope for the sexual sinner who repents. There is freedom. When the "I surrender" flag is flying and there is complete submission to the work of the Holy Spirit, men and women will be able to stand in purity and walk in holiness.

1. Summarize what you learned in this Bible study. Mark the statements below that are true for you.

   ❏ I have come to know God.
   ❏ I have come to know his love.
   ❏ I now know that God is perfect.
   ❏ I can trust his love for me.

❏ I have come to trust him with my past.
❏ I have put my trust in God's ways.
❏ I have experienced his healing.
❏ I believe his promises.
❏ I feel safe in his holy presence.
❏ I have found a place of rest for my soul.
❏ I now know where I have been sexually wounded.
❏ I understand how the things I learned about sex as a child have affected me.
❏ I understand the effect of the trauma I have experienced.
❏ I have changed my mind about sex.
❏ I have opened my heart to God's plan for my sexuality.
❏ I have changed my old clothes (attitudes and behaviors) and put on his new ones.
❏ I have turned around and I am going a new way.

2. In the space provided, write a prayer of thanksgiving for specific areas of growth and specific needs for further healing.

Group Discussion Guide

Scripture Memory Verse

> Godly sorrow brings repentance that leads to salvation and leaves no regret, but worldly sorrow brings death.
> 2 Corinthians 7:10

Discussion Questions

1. In what ways have you turned around the way you are living?
2. What was the most significant truth you applied to your life in the course of this study?
3. What do you think is your next step in furthering your healing?
4. Are there any prayer requests you would like to share?

Notes

Date:_____

Notes

Date: _____

_____
_____
_____
_____
_____
_____
_____
_____
_____
_____
_____
_____
_____
_____
_____
_____
_____
_____
_____
_____
_____
_____
_____
_____
_____
_____
_____
_____
_____
_____
_____

Notes

Date: _____

Notes

Date:_____

Notes

Date: _____

Notes

Date:_____

Notes

Date: _____

Notes

Date:_____

Notes

Date: _____